TEMPERANCE

AND

EDUCATION,

OR,

The Relation of the Social Drinking Customs to the Educational Interests of the Nation.

By Mark Hopkins, D.D.

NEW YORK:
The National Temperance Society,
No. 58 READE STREET.

1876.

MISCELLANEOUS PUBLICATIONS.

Bacchus Dethroned: a Prize Essay. By Frederick Powell $1
The Bases of the Temperance Reform. By Rev. Dawson Burns 1
Bound Volume of Sermons 1
Forty Years' Fight with the Drink Demon. By Dr. Charles Jewett 1
Drops of Water. 56 New Temperance Poems. By Ella Wheeler .....
Four Pillars of Temperance. By John W. Kirton .....
The Four Pillars are: Reason, Science, Scripture, and Experience
Alcohol: Its Nature and Effects. By Charles A. Story, M.D .....
Scripture Testimony against Intoxicating Wine. By Rev. Wm. Ritchie, of Scotland .....
Bible Rule of Temperance; or, Total Abstinence from all Intoxicating Drinks. By George Duffield, D.D .....
Alcohol: Its Place and Power. By James Miller. And the Use and Abuse of Tobacco. By John Lizars 1
Delavan's Consideration of the Temperance Argument and History 1
Temperance Anecdotes. By G. W. Bungay 1
The National Temperance Orator. By Miss L. Penney 1
The Temperance Speaker. By J. N. Stearns .....
Communion Wine and Bible Temperance. By Rev. Wm. M. Thayer. Paper, 20 cents; cloth .....
Bible Wines; or, Laws of Fermentation and Wines of the Ancients. By Rev. William Patton, D.D. Paper, 30 cents; cloth .....
Bound Volume of Tracts. Nos. 1 and 2, each 1
Text-Book of Temperance. By Dr. F. R. Lees 1
Temperance Chimes. By William B. Bradbury and J. N. Stearns. Comprising 128 pp. of Songs, Hymns, Glees, etc., set to appropriate music. Paper covers, single copies, 30 cents; $25 per 100. In board covers, single copies, 35 cents; per 100 30
Bugle Notes for the Temperance Army. By W. F. Sherwin and J. N. Stearns. 128 pp. of New and Popular Music. Paper cover, 30 cents single copy; $25 per 100. Board cover, 35 cents; per 100 30
Temperance Hymn-Book. Paper, 12 cents; boards .....
Package of Assorted Tracts. Nos. 1 and 2. 250 pp. Each .....
Package of 72 Children's Tracts .....
Packet of Prohibition Documents. 250 pp .....
Campaign Temperance Hymn-Book. 24 pp. Per 100 3

THE YOUTH'S TEMPERANCE BANNER.

The National Temperance Society and Publication House publish a beautifull illustrated Monthly Paper, especially adapted to children and youth, Sunday-Scho and Juvenile Temperance Organizations. Each number contains several choi engravings, a piece of music, and a great variety of articles from the pens of t best writers for children in America. It should be placed in the hands of eve child in the land.

The Congress of the United States has passed a law that the postage on papers sent through the mails after the 1st of January, 1875, must be paid in a vance at the office where the paper is published.

Terms, Cash in Advance, Including Postage.

Single copy, one year,	**$0 35**	Forty, to one address,	$5
Eight, to one address,	**1 08**	Fifty, " "	6
Twenty, " "	**2 70**	One hundred "	13

THE NATIONAL TEMPERANCE ADVOCATE.

The National Temperance Society and Publication House publish a ne Monthly Temperance Paper, the object of which is to promote the interests of th cause of Temperance by disseminating light from every quarter upon its more social, financial, and scientific bearings. The best talent in the land will be secure for its editors and contributors. Single copy, one year, $1 10; 10 copies, to one a dress, $10; 20 copies, to one address, $18; all ov.. 20 copies, at 90 cents per cop which includes postage. Address

J. N. STEARNS, Publishing Agent, 58 Reade St., New York.

TEMPERANCE

AND

EDUCATION;

OR,

The Relation of the Social Drinking Customs to the Educational Interests of the Nation.

BY MARK HOPKINS, D.D.

NEW YORK:
The National Temperance Society,
NO. 58 READE STREET.

1876.

[The following paper was kindly prepared by Dr. HOPKINS, by special invitation, for the opening of a series of parlor conferences or conversaziones, under the auspices of the National Temperance Society. It was read by the author on the evening of December 23, 1875, in the parlors of the Hon. WM. E. DODGE, President of the Society, and listened to with profound attention by a large number of guests, including many distinguished representatives of the professional and mercantile life of the metropolis.]

TEMPERANCE AND EDUCATION.

I AM desired to open this conversation by some remarks on "the relation of the social drinking customs to the educational interests of the nation."

This, I suppose, I am asked to do from my long connection with education. It is just fifty years this autumn since I first went to Williams College as an instructor, and, with the exception of three years, I have been there since—

thirty-six years as president. For several years I was the oldest president in office in the country. I may be supposed, therefore, to know something about education; but about the drinking customs of society I know very little; and to treat a double subject of this sort well it would seem necessary to know both parts of it. But I have no statistics; I have collected no facts. The evils of intemperance I have known, but how far they have originated in social drinking customs I have not known.

I remember well the first movement in Williamstown and in the college on the subject of temperance. It was, I think, as early as 1832 or 1833. There were two hotels in the place, both selling liquor as a matter of course, and three or four stores that retailed several hogsheads each annually. No one seemed to suppose the traffic wrong. But one Sabbath Dr. Hewitt, then of Bridgeport, preached two tremendous sermons on the subject; and now note the effect of a trained conscience when it is enlightened. The next day both hotels and every store in town stopped selling. I have never known such an effect produced by any discourse, or any two discourses, before or since. The effect of those discourses is felt in the town to this day. A public sentiment was created that has never died out. For a long time the traffic was wholly suppressed, and has never been resumed in the stores since.

Dr. Griffin, then president of the college, a grand man, six feet four inches high and well proportioned, fond of a good dinner, and accustomed to have wine with it, gave up his wine at once. A society was formed in the college, and what could be done by moral suasion was done. After that, attention was drawn to the evils of drinking in the college as it had not been before; and since that time it has not ceased to be watched and guarded against. At one time the trustees passed a law requiring every student entering college to pledge himself not to use intoxicating drink during term-time and on college ground. This law was in force for a number of years, but it was found that the consciences of students—many of them, at least — were very elastic in regard to a pledge which they regarded as enforced; and the attempt to isolate the college by placing it under a different social law from that of the general community was abandoned.

The fact that the college could not be thus isolated shows two things. It shows the community of interest that runs through all parts of the social fabric, as through an organized body. This community of interest must always exist in some degree, but it becomes fuller and more vital as intelligence and the power of the press and facilities of intercourse are increased. The fact that we cannot thus isolate a college shows also that we cannot treat this subject of drinking customs and their effects in a satisfactory way if we regard as education simply that which is technically so called.

By education we commonly mean that process for which special provision is made in teachers, and buildings, and books, and apparatus, and which has for its object to fit young persons for their posi-

tions in life. But there is a broader view. Taking the term in its wider sense, it will include everything that has exerted a formative influence, and has caused a young person to be, at a given point, what he is.

If we place before us a young man, say of twenty-one, whose education is said to be completed, and technically is so, we ask, the community ask, respecting him, two questions. One is, What is he? and the other is, What can he do? What is he in his character, his principles, his disposition, his habits, his tendencies? What can he do? Can he plead a cause, or keep books, or build a bridge or a railroad, or run one? These two questions we ask, and according to our answer to them we estimate the prospects of the young man.

If now we ask how he came to be what he is, and to be able to do what he can do, we shall need to consider four things. One is the constitution and tendencies he inherited from his parents; the second is the family and social influences by which he was surrounded; the third is formal teaching in schools and colleges, commonly called education; and the fourth is that inscrutable will-power that belongs to every rational and accountable being, through which he is able to modify or control results, whatever the original constitution, or social influences, or positive instruction may have been.

Of the great influence of the first of these—inherited constitution and tendencies—there can be no doubt. God seems to have arranged the constitution of the race in a way to bring the most powerful influences possible to bear on those who were to perpetuate it to do what they could to improve it, or at least not to deteriorate it. It may seem hard that the iniquities of the parents should be visited on the children; but in no other way could the laws of temperance be so powerfully enforced. Let parents see, as they must, that not only constitutions generally puny and feeble are inherited, but also a tendency to consumption, a tendency to insanity, a tendency to drunkenness, and the whole power of parental affection, as well as of self-interest, will work to dissuade them from any form of vicious indulgence. It is not, you will observe, the consumption, or the insanity, or the drunkenness that is inherited, but the *tendency* to these. That tendency may or may not be overcome. There the will-power may come in; but the child enters upon life under conditions far less favorable than it would otherwise. If intemperate parents could blast only their own lives, and have it stop there, it would be comparatively little; but to send needless weakness, and exposure, and degradation down to successive generations is fearful. To do this for the sake of any temporary pleasure is like the wickedness lately discovered of putting an infernal machine on board a steamer that would blow it up in mid-ocean for the sake of the insurance.

Looking, then, at our supposed young man, we cannot doubt the great influence upon him, both in what he is and in what he can do, of his inherited constitution and tendencies. But as these were originally given, and could not be affected by us, they need not be considered further

We pass, then, to the family social influences under which he has been placed. These have surrounded him as an atmosphere, and, the constitution being given, are undoubtedly the most constant, pervasive, efficient, and moulding of all external influence in causing him *to be* what he is. I hold on to the distinction between *being* and *doing;* and these, I say, are the influences most likely to have been efficient in causing him *to be* what he is. So God intended it should be. For the same reason that he has established the law of heredity, by which the parents become responsible for the constitution of the child as it is born into life, has he established what may be called a law of social heredity, by which the family becomes responsible for what he shall be at his second birth into society. By a natural law which he will not abrogate, God visits the iniquities of the fathers upon the children. By a similar law, identical in principle, he visits the iniquities of families upon society; and through both these laws he is constantly uttering to men the broader law announced by our Saviour: "Make the tree good, and the fruit will be good." Do men gather grapes of thorns or figs of thistles? The family is God's institution, and so he honors and guards it. He intended it should be the seed-plot of society. Let all the families in a community be what they should be, and the community will be what it should be. This is according to the natural course of things; and then we have the promise of God for it: "Train up a child"—a *child*, observe, not a lad of a dozen years or a miss in her teens, but a *child*—"in the way he should go, and when he is old he will not depart from it." Childhood, early childhood, is the formative, the flexible, the impressible period. If the mind of a child can go through with all the processes by which it learns a language before it is four years old, it must also be possible to implant in it guiding principles that shall go with it through life.

The training spoken of will imply more than teaching. It implies a settled, definite purpose and time given to its accomplishment. It implies example as well as precept. It will include the set, the drift, the animus, the general spirit, of the family. Let the spirit of the family be one of industry, economy, kindness, cheerfulness, temperance, purity, liberality, and godliness, and the promise of God will be made good, however unfavorable the circumstances may be by which they are surrounded. When three young men, more than three thousand years ago, were cast into a burning fiery furnace, they were not in favorable circumstances, but they came out with no smell of fire upon them. What more unfavorable circumstances than for a large family of boys, with no sister to exert any refining or restraining influence, to be brought up in a large city, surrounded by every form of temptation, knowing that their father had wealth, and that they were to have it; and yet I have known a family of seven boys brought up to manhood in that way, and the promise not fail in regard to one of them. The Bible does not say that if a child is not trained up in the way he should go he shall never get into it.

There are formative influences outside the family, and there are the will-power and the Spirit of God to help; but, as in the case of heredity, the tendencies will be in the wrong direction.

As I have said, one main thing in training is the set, the drift, and general spirit of the family and of the social elements around them. Let a young man rightly trained go to a literary institution *from such a family as I have indicated,* and he will be almost sure neither to be a promoter of disorder nor to fall into intemperate habits. In all my experience I have never known an instance, where I was sure the training had been right, in which a young man has thus fallen. If all young men going into our literary institutions were to be thus trained, the institutions could not fail of being what they should be. Suppose, on the other hand, that the majority of the young men go from families, reputable indeed, but worldly, fashionable, selfish, self-indulgent, accustomed to the use of wine and other forms of nervous stimulation, having, perhaps, associated the use of wine with gentility, and the exclusion of it and of drinking customs generally with fanaticism and narrowness; and it is as certain as any law of nature that there will be occasional disgraceful disorder among the young men, and that numbers will form habits of drinking that will carry them down to drunkards' graves. Instructors may preach, and exhort, and set up what barriers they please; the young men are fortified against anything they can do by *filial piety itself*, to say nothing of incipient appetite and the begun work of the deceiver. God never meant that families should sink down into disregard of him and disobedience of his laws, and then be able to set up a system of outside institutions that should make their children what they ought to be. Parents are willing to pay money—oh! yes; but the gift of God in the results of parental faithfulness cannot be purchased with money.

It is precisely at this point that the drinking customs of a country will bear upon its educational interests. They will ensure, to a greater or less extent, the use of intoxicating drinks in our literary institutions. Whatever may be said of such use elsewhere and in other connections, as connected with education the effect is evil.

In an address, two years and more ago, before the National Temperance Convention at Saratoga, which I gave, as I now do this, at the request of the President of the National Temperance Society, I stated and illustrated the following points in regard to the young generally:

1st. That neither alcoholic drinks nor narcotics of any kind are needed at that period of life, either for the upbuilding of the system or for enjoyment.

2d. That during this period these substances are especially injurious and dangerous — injurious from their effect upon the physical system in its formative period; dangerous, first, from the deceptive character of these stimulants, especially for the inexperienced; and, secondly, because it is the period of the ready formation of habits, and of habits that are also artificial appetites. It is to the power of habit that the fearful dominion of these substances over men is generally ascribed. It is not wholly or even chiefly that. It is from that, in connection with a craving artificially produced, that is really of the nature of a disease, and which often so becomes a disease as to require medical treatment and special asylums.

3d. It was observed that those who least need artificial stimulants are in the most danger from them. Nervous persons, gifted persons, those of poetical temperament and special promise, are more likely than others to become the victims of artificial stimulation.

So much for the young generally. In regard to those who devote themselves to study, some things were mentioned as peculiar.

1st. The life is sedentary, and not in the open air. Hence less power to resist or counteract the influence of narcotics and artificial stimulants.

2d. That in his proper work a student has no use for his muscles, but must so use his brain as to draw from them blood and nervous energy. Hence the need of avoiding everything that will impair the digestive functions or lower the tone of muscular power, as narcotics and artificial stimulants are known to do.

3d. That life in our educational institutions is social in such a way that there is special danger through the social nature that drinking habits will be formed.

4th. That the effect of these substances is wholly antagonistic to that control of the voluntary over the involuntary powers of the mind which it is one great object of education to give.

If these propositions can be maintained — and I am sure that every one of them can — it must follow that the whole influence upon the educational interests of the country of intoxicating drinks, and so of the drinking customs of society, is evil.

In closing, I desire to say that I agree with Dr. Edmunds, of London, in saying, as he recently did in his excellent addresses in this city, that whatever is physiologically right is morally right. That doctrine I have always held. In the addresses at Saratoga already referred to, I went so far as to say that if stimulation by alcohol, or tobacco, or opium, or arsenic would enable us to reach the highest state of balanced power, physical, intellectual, moral, spiritual, then we are not only at liberty to use those substances, but are bound to do it. This I say. But I go further, and say that whatever is physiologically wrong is morally wrong. We have no right to do ourselves harm. No man has a right to make his body an instrument of pleasure in such a way as to lower its tone or derange its functions, or in any way unfit it for those higher uses to which it may be put in the service of the rational spirit. Let men so use their bodies as best to serve the interests of their higher powers, and I am content.

www.ingramcontent.com/pod-product-compliance
Lightning Source LLC
LaVergne TN
LVHW011126110826
845150LV00008B/2264

* 9 7 8 1 4 1 8 1 9 5 1 3 7 *